Love, Brooke

Brooklyn E. Wilson

www.mascotbooks.com

Love, Brooke

For more information, please contact:
Mascot Books
620 Herndon Parkway, Suite 320
Herndon, VA 20170
info@mascotbooks.com

Library of Congress Control Number: 2019911218

CPSIA Code: PRFRE1019A
ISBN: 978-1-64307-536-5

Printed in Canada

dedicated to those who know what love is, those who don't, and those who wish to know. those who've felt every bit of love, every bit of heartache, every bit of regret, every bit of happiness, every bit of sorrow, and every bit of struggle. this is for you. please, feel every word. cry, smile, and reminisce. let your emotions breathe.

preface

when you feel so full of love all the time...you feel like you have no choice
but to let it burst, to let it spill from your heart and through your fingers
as you write letters and letters. letters to your lover. letters to yourself.
letters to your friends. love feels like every emotion crashing together
all at once. love is joyful. love is draining. love is overwhelming. love
is anger. love is bittersweet. love is unconditional. love is soulful. love
is beautiful, romantic, and platonic. It's a natural feeling we can't get
rid of. we, as humans, should not allow love to completely break us. It
can...and it will at times, but allow it to heal you as well. don't be afraid
of what is has done in the past. love will always open a door to a new
beginning. every wound needs a little love. love someone. love yourself.
love your surroundings. just love. love will always be worth feeling.

point in time

there was a point in time
when I loved you
more than I loved myself.
now,
it's the other way around.
and
I can't believe I ever gave you,
someone who was not worthy,
that kind of power.
that was my fault.
you never deserved it.

to the victims of sexual assault.

I admire you for so many reasons. your strength is unmatchable. you are the most deserving of love and happiness. the courage you have and your willingness to face pain, fear, and uncertainty is beyond inspiring. you are remarkable and you have all of my respect. I can only imagine being in your shoes. I can only imagine being as powerful as you are. please don't forget to protect your spirit. protect yourself. you are human and your body is yours. take care of your body. you were created for no one other than yourself. be proud of yourself and be proud of how far you've come. new doors are opening. new chapters are beginning for you; chapters filled with endless recovery, healing, growth, love, and self-discovery. keep moving forward and don't look back. you've made it so far and you deserve to keep going. you deserve to flourish, and you will. thank yourself for being so strong. love yourself. take care.

"you can't love anyone else if you can't love yourself"

don't listen to people
who try to feed you lies
such as
"you can't love anyone else
if you struggle loving yourself."
remind yourself
that this is far from true.
you are more than capable
of expressing love, appreciation, and admiration
even if you are incapable
of providing yourself with such treatment.

artists

artists
remember to
put all your emotions into your craft.
put your all in
and let your voice crack
when you sing.
let the music control your body
when you dance.
break down and cry, or laugh and smile
when you write.
plant every creative idea on your canvas
when you draw.
let yourself **feel.**
you are your art.

force.

you can't force anything
that isn't right for you.
things need to come naturally
at their own pace.
you can't force anyone to love you,
be honest with you,
or appreciate you.
see things as they are
and know when enough is enough.
know when the loyalty isn't there.
know when they aren't accepting of you.
you can't force things that can't be saved.
open your eyes and let things flow.
be honest with yourself.

blinded

why did you allow yourself
to become blinded by infatuation and lust?
why did you allow yourself
to believe that it was anything
close to love?
something won't allow me
to drift away from you...
but trust me when I say
I want to.
I want you to realize
how it feels to have me removed
from your life for just a second.
I know you don't deserve me
but I like to convince myself that you do.
I hope you open your eyes.
I can only pray for someone
as blinded as you are.

a letter for the boy who I will love next:

I will love you hardcore. my love is by far the "'til death do us part" type of love. you could try to search for my love in someone else, but you will fail at finding it. I'll love you as if this is still the honeymoon stage years later. I will practically give you my heart because I know it is safe in your hands. I will pour all my love onto you with no warning, but please be prepared. I will want to know all of your secrets that you have hidden deep and wouldn't dare let slip from your lips. I will want to know all your fears. I will want to know all the trauma that you've been through just so I can be aware as to what shaped you into who you are today. I will be clingy, but I will also give you freedom—just please do not betray me. instead, reassure me. I will be emotional over little things. I will take every gesture and every word to the heart. do not tell me that you love me but refuse to show me. I will not take that very well. I will have trouble being so open naturally. because of this you'll have to pull it out of me. know that I am a pro when it comes to distancing myself when I feel hurt, when I feel neglected, when I feel as if I'm being a bother. please know that all I need is some reassurance. I will always need reassurance. some days my insecurities will greet me and they will cause me to feel like anything but myself. please bear with me. know that I am goofy and weirder than most. know that once I start laughing, I don't stop. know that I will laugh at things that are far from funny so there's no need to tell me. know that I am lighthearted and I will always accept you for who you are. so please, do not hide from me. know that I have quite a few things that I need to work on. know that I am always growing and that I am always working on ways to better myself. know that even though I am working on so many things, I will never have to work on loving you, because loving you is already set and done. I am not hard to love, not hard at all. I may be overwhelming and more passionate than you might be used to, but darling know that it is worth it. because in the end, we'll both know that my love was always true.

permission

I need
permission to love you
as hard as I naturally can;
permission to love you
with a deep burning passion;
permission to love you
until I'm genuinely exhausted.
I would hate to scare you
with my level of intensity.
so please, be aware of what you're getting
yourself into and reassure me
that I will not overwhelm you.
give me permission.

what I'd teach my son:

1. be gentle. be as gentle as you possibly can. don't let society cloud your mind with thoughts that just because you are a certain gender, you must act a certain way. don't let hypermasculinity overpower you. act the way you feel. act the way that is you.

2. cry. be emotional. let everything you're feeling pour out before you can even allow it. don't think twice. release toxic energy and embrace positive energy. give yourself permission to feel.

3. no means no. do not force yourself upon anyone for any reason and do not let anyone force themselves onto you. do not believe that you own anyone despite the relationship you two might have. do not ignore that you are making someone uncomfortable. do not become deaf to the cries for your own benefit. no. means. no.

4. love is love. love who you want. I promise I will not judge you. I promise you will be safe in your own home regardless of who you may love. let your heart open up and let your love be free.

5. there will never be a day when you are not being supported. do what you want. be who you want to be. say what you want to say. you are beautiful. you are worthy. you are loved. you are everything that I could ever want and need. I love you.

self-love

self-love is separating your wellbeing
from anything it doesn't agree with. providing yourself with harmony
and taking care of your spirit. be patient with your growth and don't force
yourself to be perfect. remove toxicity and heal at a pace that is comfortable.
as corny as it may sound, everything will be okay. It's necessary that you
remind yourself of that. keep up with yourself and reward yourself. be proud
of yourself. love yourself and practice self-care whenever you get the chance.

my favorite book

you're my favorite book and I can't wait to read every chapter.
I want to flip through your pages and take in every word.
I want to figure out why you act the way you do;
what can trigger the anger you have built up inside of you.
I want to know your more lighthearted aspects;
what can bring you to your most content state.
I always notice myself gravitating towards you.
the wisdom associated with your words
reeled me in and I stayed for more.
I aspire to comprehend every piece of you no matter
the amount of time it takes up.
give me all the scattered pieces that make up your puzzle
and let me put them together.
I promise I won't judge you once the hidden picture is revealed.
I promise I won't be frightened by the traumas and fears
one chapter caused;
traumas superglued to your mind that you can't get rid of;
fears that haunt you from dusk 'til dawn.

let me feel what you felt when you experienced what you did.
allow me to read your background story thoroughly,
without neglecting any of your supporting details.
reading between the lines helped me see the bigger picture.
you suffer with your past.
you have trouble with dealing with your emotions.
you're tired of trying. you wish you still had hope.
your heart has been broken up into these tiny pieces
that you never picked up and put back into place.
if you can't, can I?
can I be the love interest that you're missing throughout your storyline,
if you don't mind?
I've noticed your past lovers were masked antagonists
pretending to love you, thus being the reasoning
for your countless chapters of heartbreak.
so please,
let me be the reason your story took a plot twist
and ended happily.

a love letter

to the one who started it all. you were the beginning of this self-love journey. I thank you for putting me on track. I didn't know how to love myself. I refused to face my flaws. I didn't think I'd ever accept myself, until you left. I loved you more than I loved myself. I was willing to accept your imperfections and mistakes, but I resented myself because of mine. you taught me to never put anyone above myself. you let me know that I can't expect others to carry my insecurities on their back. you left just as quick as you came, but I've come to peace with you. I still have a great amount of love for you. you've become one of the most important people in my life, and what you taught me will stay with me forever. thank you for the lessons.

to the one who gave me the first glimpse of what love was. the love I grew for you was intense. it brought tears of joy, sadness, and anger. you taught me how to let go; to leave when necessary no matter how much it hurts; to know my worth and never settle for less. you taught me how to be patient; how to live in the moment. your lessons brought the most pain, but it will always be worth it. I love you dearly. thank you for the lessons.

to the one who came without warning; the one who made me feel safe without even trying because your presence was the most comforting; the one who really tried to understand me; the one willing to grow with me but still allowing me the space I need: thank you for the love. thank you for always making everything better. thank you for trying. we aren't perfect, but it's okay. you are so appreciated.

to all of the boys i've ever loved, I am so grateful for you. I hold every single one of you dear to my heart. thank you for the happiness, the tears, and the lessons. I've loved and I've lost, but what I received in the end will always be remembered.

how?

I wrote about you
every second I could,
putting a pen to paper
and explaining
how you made my heart
beat a little faster.
that was my happy place.
I still write about you
except
I explain how you made my heart cry out.
my heart was screaming
but you were too deaf
to hear the calls.
I wasted such precious words on you.
how sad.
I read back and wonder
how everything went so bad.

control

I let my emotions take over
when I feel too weak to be in charge.
letting my emotions release
is like waves
crashing into each other
dangerously, unsteadily.
I lose strength
trying to keep myself up,
leaving me no choice
but to fall and drown in it all.
I often end up restless
but rejuvenated
once all the damage is done.

role play

I've learnt not to be
resentful of those
who walked out of my life
but to instead be grateful.
they weren't meant
to be in my space
and I've taught myself
to be okay with it.
they played their role
and they quit.
preparing me for someone
who will play their role
and stick to it.

sunsets

sunsets.
I love to study the way the sky can shift,
admiring the variety of tints the sky creates.
different shades of pinks, oranges,
and purples dripping into one another
like a watercolor painting in the making.
I make sure I capture these moments.
they help remind me that there is so much to appreciate,
that there is plenty of beauty hidden in this world.
finding it is easy
if you take a second to recognize it.

12/28/02

I can't wait for you to grow up and see what I have, meet the people I've met, learn the things that will help you along this journey. your determination to live a happy life will stick with you. you will learn independence early. you will be so inspiring to others. your talents will be recognized, and you will have such a special way with words. your happiness will set people free and your empathy will bring them in. you will have people who will try to dim your light and...you will let them. at some point you'll go through a time deciding whether you should love or hate yourself, but you will choose love. you will be more sensitive than others but you'll be resilient. your feelings will be fragile, but you'll learn to block negativity out of your life. people will tell you that you're "too much." too sensitive, too emotional, too weird, too pushy, too focused on your work, too quiet, but you won't listen to them. you'll know anyone who doesn't appreciate you for you isn't meant to be in your space. I'm so proud of the young woman you are now. I am so proud of the strength and knowledge you've gained, the things you've taught yourself, the people you've decided to admire, the way you handle things, how patient you are with yourself. I'm proud of US. don't let anything hinder your growth. learn from your mistakes and prosper. I love you more than you know.

—A message to little me

moving on

I knew I had moved on
when seeing you with her
no longer felt like the world
was crashing down on me.
it no longer left a bitter taste in my mouth.
seeing you with her didn't hurt anymore.
instead, I was relieved.
instead I felt at peace knowing that
I was no longer yours.
I didn't have to deal with your childish ways anymore.
instead I hoped that you'd treat her better than you ever treated me.
please, treat her better.
I hope you've matured.
I wish you well.

better is coming.

if it disrupts your peace
and takes you
out of your safe place,
it is **not** meant for you.
remove yourself
and wait for the better.

restrictions.

It's not possible
for me to feel
without expressing,
whether the whole world listens
or nobody at all.
letting go is easy.
the restrictions are what drive me crazy.

broken

I'm not attracted to a soul with no darkness hidden somewhere. it's something about a damaged soul that interests me more than anything. their eyes have millions of stories to tell. read into them and you'll be hooked. their twisted minds have reasoning behind every deadly thought. their broken hearts have love waiting to burst...but they're afraid they'll burst just a little too much only to end up scarred in the end. they're afraid of what loving again could possibly do. they're afraid of healing, because they are so sure they'll just break and crumble all over again. they're afraid of being optimistic. they know the worst is creeping up on them as they try to take steps towards the best. they break those who had no intention of breaking them. they bruise the hearts of those who only wished to mend their wounds. they have demons fighting against them, but they soon gave up on trying to win that battle. they're full of pain—pain ready to be taken out on everyone else because they don't want to be alone in this. they don't want to feel like life is only going wrong on their end. somehow, all of this does nothing but reel me in. it makes me wonder. what beauty hides behind this ugly mask? what can you find if you search through their many layers? what is the plot in their story? why are they so sick and detached? the broken and the damaged: this is what I am attracted to.

mind vs. heart

I never write from my mind
or else I'd be expressing
bitter, guarded emotions
that I **want** to believe.
I write from my heart
expressing only raw, vulnerable emotions
that I have **no choice** but to believe.

power

I let love overpower me. I get lost in love when it consumes me. It is so easy for me to let my guard down, but so hard at the same time. I search for love in the most subtle way possible, but when it approaches me, I run. I search for someone who adores me. but when they finally introduce themselves, I run. I search for someone who understands me, but when they do, I run. I shut down. I run because I'm not ready. I'm not ready to put someone else above myself again. I'm not ready to temporarily forget what balance is because I'd rather tend to someone else's needs than tend to my own. I shut down because catching feelings all over again before I even have a chance to say stop is just something I'd rather not do. I let love come in and take over. I let love build me up higher and higher. I let love crush me once it's all over. I'm beginning to know my worth. I'm beginning to tell the difference between what I want from love versus what I need from it. I'm beginning to listen to my intuition and admit to myself when something is not right for me. I'm used to running from my lessons. I'm used to looking the truth dead in its eyes but still being blind to it. I'm beginning to open my eyes. growth. find me and transform me into the woman I need to be. the woman who prefers her needs over her wants. the woman who searches for love from herself before she looks anywhere else. the woman who faces love with vulnerability. but is strong enough to say no when love attempts to crush her all over again.

soul ties

have I ever told you
how much I cherish your hugs?
I could hug you for hours and hours
and still feel incomplete when you pull away.
I don't care how corny or cliché this may sound,
but when you hug me, we're suddenly
the only two people in the room.
everyone else disappears
for a second and it's just us.
it's just you.
I don't care who's watching.
I don't care about the eyewitnesses
because in that moment
holding on to you is my only concern.
I don't receive your hugs often
but when I finally get the chance, the feeling I get is almost indescribable.
you have a touch that makes me feel like
I'm becoming one with you.
you have a touch that makes me feel safe.
you are so warm.
you've always made me feel cozy
and I love it.
I find a hug the sweetest way to say "I love you,"
so if I could hug you all day I definitely would,
just so you can know that
I love you more than words can say.

rise

practice manifesting. speak love into your life. be honest with what
you want. have good intentions. have respect for others and demand it
back. treat people with kindness and wish them the best if they don't
return it. don't take your irritation out on people. don't expect others
to deal with your problems because you don't want to. don't make
permanent decisions based on temporary anger. protect your energy and
don't carry hate in your heart—for yourself or anybody else. rise above
those who are below you. keep in mind that pain is only temporary.
you are better than anything holding you back. remember that.

how to love me

1. know that my heart is as soft as a cloud. be as gentle as you can with me. know that my feelings are overwhelming, but please, don't distance yourself from me. know that I will love you until I can't anymore. know that I will pour my soul into you...and that it will be heavy. I just hope... that you're strong enough. know that I'm a whole package...but I promise, I will deliver my love to you in a way you'll never forget.

2. be my best friend before, during, and after you are my partner. show me that you care enough to never allow what we have to slip from your heart. let us have a bond that has been built with love. let us witness each other grow mentally and physically. if we were to ever end, please don't become a stranger.

3. hugs that feel like home. forehead kisses that make me feel cherished. cuddles that make me feel safe and snug. pulling each other in no matter how close...because we just wish to be closer. holding hands. gazing into my eyes. physical affection and intimacy...this is my love language.

4. do not grow annoyed with me when I blast the same song nonstop. instead, listen with me. be willing to sit through a marathon of Disney movies as I reminisce on how these same movies made me so happy as a young girl. allow me to teach you about the study of astrology and do not make me feel odd when I ask you about your time of birth. let me know that you care about the little things that I show a great deal of interest in.

5. just let me love you. don't make me feel bad for how passionate I am. don't make me feel like my love is too much to handle. don't make me feel like I need to tone it down because I'm getting way too ahead of myself. don't make me feel like my clinginess is a flaw. understand this is the way I am. just please...let me love you the way I know how to.

adolescent

love can seem like a fairytale when you experience it young.
you feel like that person is the only one who can birth happiness in your heart.
you look at them and become so enthralled that you don't even notice anyone
or anything else. you think about them so often that it's almost impossible to
focus on anything other than them.
you babble on and on about them to whomever, whether they care or not.
this is the stage when love feels perfect.
it feels so good to love someone.
you know it might sound crazy saying you can't live without them,
but you wonder how crazy you could possibly sound.
they give you endless butterflies every time you see them.
every time they lock eyes with you. every time their lips union with yours.
something as simple as holding your hand and you'd never want it to end
because their touch gives you this tingle that you love so much.
love itself is so beautiful but loving during
the adolescent years can really make you feel like
dreams do come true.

infatuation

Infatuation can disguise itself
as love.
It can confuse the heart,
confuse the mind.
It makes you feel like
you've found the one
when really,
you've only found your next lesson.

brooklyn

I'm learning how to love myself, how to feel confident. I'm being honest
with myself about what I can and can't change. I'm accepting my flaws. I've
learned to appreciate the things I once neglected. I'm letting myself live.
I remind myself that it's okay to be human, that insecurities are normal,
but they don't define me. my imperfections are perfect, and I've fallen
in love with them. I am comfortable in my own body. I'm comfortable
with who I am: my big brown eyes, my wide smile, my somewhat
curly hair, my tiny hands, my sense of style, the way I talk, my terrible
eyesight, my huge glasses…I love it all. this is my skin, my body, my face.
I've learned how to take care of myself. I've realized that self-love is a
lifelong journey. I always waited for the day I'd wake up and love myself.
I didn't know it didn't work that way. I realized I had to decide when this
journey started…and I've decided. I've learned how to love myself.

just a reminder

1. you're worthy of love—love of every kind. you deserve to feel loved. don't accept anything less.

2. you are not hard to love. you carry a lot of passion. you carry so much in that heart of yours, but one day the package you carry won't be difficult for someone else to pick up.

3. you bring light into this world. you are here for a reason. don't leave. stay.

4. you woke up today. today is another day that came with a chance to start over; a chance to heal. take that chance. take that opportunity.

5. it's okay not to be okay. it's okay to lose yourself. it's okay to drown yourself in your own tears. it's okay to break down, as long as you bring yourself back up. take as long as you need. come back stronger, calmer, and happier.

6. you CAN talk to someone. someone out there will understand. talk to someone if you're comfortable. someone will listen.

7. you are beautiful. remember that.

8. this is your life. make it what you want it. don't let anyone turn your life into theirs.

9. you will be okay. you will be loved. you will find love within yourself. you will be strong.

10. you are PERFECT the way you are—I mean it. be honest with yourself and don't alter yourself for anyone. love yourself even if they don't love you.

the last poem.

thank you, for loving me. you loved every piece of me, not caring how long it would take for me to love it as well. you helped me figure out so many things about myself. you have helped me to see myself in such a better light. you taught me how to be patient. you taught me to live in the moment and to hope for the future. you taught me not to rush love. thank you. they say the people who walk into your life will either be a blessing or a lesson. but you—you were both. that is why I will forever hold you dear to my heart. I will hold everything about you...dear to my heart. everything that makes you, you are more than beautiful. I love all the battle scars that rest in your soul; the scars that make you stronger every given day. I love your heart that's oh-so-damaged; a heart that's been broken...so many times. yet, the love you spread to those who love you will forever be so full. you have a love that is your own. you have a love that is unmatched. I love the moments where you're smiling and being unapologetically yourself just as much as the moments where you feel like giving up. the moments where you lose yourself and feel like you aren't worthy. you have so many imperfections, but I will always love each and every one of them more than anything. thank you for being so special. thank you for showing me that I am not hard to love. thank you for showing me that it is possible for me to be understood. thank you for allowing yourself to allow me, to love you. you'll always have a piece of my heart in some way, shape, or form. you're someone I thank God for every day. you're my best friend and I thank you—for it all.

Acknowledgments

1. God

2. everyone who's ever supported me. everyone who bought a book. my family and my friends. thank you for believing in me and encouraging me to believe in myself. I love you.